THE DEATHSTALKER SCORPION

BY LISA OWINGS

BELLWETHER MEDIA • MINNEAPOLIS, MN

Jump into the cockpit and take flight with Pilot books. Your journey will take you on high-energy adventures as you learn about all that is wild, weird, fascinating, and fun!

This edition first published in 2013 by Bellwether Media, Inc.

Library of Congress Cataloging-in-Publication Data

Owings, Lisa.
The deathstalker scorpion / by Lisa Owings.
pages cm. - (Pilot. Nature's deadliest)
Audience: 8-12.
Includes bibliographical references and index.
Summary: "Fascinating images accompany information about the deathstalker scorpion. The combination of high-interest subject matter and narrative text is intended for students in grades 3 through 7" -Provided by publisher.
ISBN 978-1-60014-879-8 (hardcover : alk. paper)
1. Leiurus quinquestriatus-Juvenile literature. 2. Scorpions-Juvenile literature. I. Title.
QL458.72.B8O95 2013
595.4'6-dc23

2012035264

Printed in the United States of America, North Mankato, MN.

CONTENTS

Sting Operation

United States Staff Sergeant Monique Munro-Harris was a long way from home in November 2006. She had been sent to Iraq to help repair medical equipment with the 506th Expeditionary Medical Squadron. One evening after work, Monique stayed up late to watch a football game on TV. Soon she was struggling to keep her eyes open. She drifted off to sleep before the game was over.

Monique woke up when she felt something crawl over her left ear. She reached up to brush it away and felt a sharp sting on her finger. Still half asleep, Monique barely reacted to the pain. Then she felt another sting on her side. This one jolted her awake. She shot out of bed and jumped around wildly to shake off her attacker. Once calm, Monique found a small scorpion on the floor.

Monique was starting to feel strange. Her throat felt tight, and breathing was difficult. Her hands began to shake. Soon she lost **consciousness**. The base hospital didn't have the **antivenom** that could save Monique. It was available at only one other hospital in the country. To get there, Monique would have to survive a 45-minute helicopter flight over enemy territory.

Halfway through the flight, Monique took a turn for the worse. Her heart nearly stopped. The medical team was able to keep her alive, but just barely. Monique received antivenom soon after landing at the hospital. However, doctors worried that she had already suffered permanent brain damage. Monique didn't wake up until several hours later. She was confused and in pain, but it was clear she would make a full recovery.

Monique Munro-Harris

After the Attack

Monique returned to her job as soon as she was healed. She received a warm welcome and a new nickname, "Scorpion Queen."

Small but Deadly

Scorpions are **arachnids** with stingers at the tips of their curved tails. They survive in forests, grasslands, mountains, caves, and many other habitats throughout the world. All scorpions are **venomous**. However, only about 25 of the more than 1,500 species are deadly to humans.

Among the most dangerous is the deathstalker. This 4-inch (10-centimeter) scorpion lives in the deserts of Africa and Asia. There it **burrows** into the sand or hides under rocks to escape the heat of the day. Its yellow color helps it blend in with its surroundings. In the cool night air, the deathstalker hunts for food. It does not need to eat often. When it does, it can consume up to one-third of its body weight.

deathstalker scorpion

paper clip

deathstalker scorpion territory = ▭

Super Survivors

- A deathstalker scorpion can survive up to a year without food.
- The deathstalker might live its whole life without drinking water. It gets most of its fluids from its prey's insides.
- Some scorpions can recover after being frozen for weeks.
- The deathstalker can stand temperatures of up to 117 degrees Fahrenheit (47 degrees Celsius).
- Some scorpions can survive underwater for up to two days.

A hungry deathstalker waits for a meal to wander close. Then the scorpion attacks. It darts out and grabs the prey with its narrow **pincers**. Its tail is curled and ready to strike. If the prey is large or puts up a fight, the deathstalker snaps its tail forward. The stinger pierces the victim. Then deadly **venom** begins to course through its body. Soon the prey is **paralyzed**. It's dinnertime for the deathstalker.

The scorpion's pincers hold its meal while its mouthparts go to work. They chew the prey while special fluids turn the animal's insides into liquid. The deathstalker sucks the liquid into its stomach. Parts of the prey that are too tough to eat are formed into a ball and spit out.

Family Dinner

Deathstalker scorpions live alone for a good reason. They tend to eat one another if given the chance. Female deathstalkers sometimes eat their mates or young.

Deathstalker venom is also powerful enough to kill humans. The **lethal** mixture is designed to attack the **nervous system**. A deathstalker does not usually **inject** enough venom to kill a healthy adult. Its sting causes pain and swelling that can last a couple of days. However, some human victims are not so lucky.

Children are the most likely to die from a deathstalker sting. The amount of venom injected is more than their small bodies can handle. Unhealthy or sensitive adults are also at risk. A severe reaction to deathstalker venom involves the whole body. Some victims shake uncontrollably. Others become weak and unable to move. Soon the heart and lungs begin to shut down. If the victim does not get antivenom quickly, death is almost certain.

Deathstalker Scorpion Attacks

Deathstalker scorpions are known for being **aggressive**. They are quick to sting if they feel threatened or trapped. Female deathstalkers also attack to protect their young. You can avoid being stung by paying attention to your surroundings. Find out if deathstalkers or other dangerous scorpions are common where you live. If so, check regularly for scorpions in and around your home. Use an **ultraviolet** flashlight to look for them. They glow under this type of light.

deathstalker scorpion under ultraviolet light

Always wear shoes when outdoors in scorpion territory. Long clothing and gloves add extra protection. Check carefully for scorpions before you reach under or grab logs or stones. If you spot a scorpion outdoors, leave it alone. A scorpion in or near your home is a bigger problem. Use tongs to pick it up. Then carefully move it to a safe area.

Hide and Seek

Scorpions are good at hiding. Here are some of their favorite places:

- **under trash heaps or garbage cans**
- **under wood piles or logs**
- **under stones or bricks**
- **under low bushes**
- **inside unworn shoes**

Stay calm if you notice a scorpion crawling on you. Gently brush it off with a nearby object or a covered part of your body. If the scorpion stings you, pay attention to what it looks like. Trap the scorpion in a container if you can. Then wash the sting with soap and water. Keep the area cool to help reduce pain and swelling.

Seek medical help if you think you were stung by a deathstalker or other dangerous scorpion. If you experience severe symptoms, it is important to act fast. Call 911 or get to a hospital immediately. If you were able to trap the scorpion, bring it with you. Your doctors will be able to identify the scorpion and give you the appropriate treatment.

Not Sure What Stung You?

You can call your local poison control center to find out if a sting could be life-threatening.

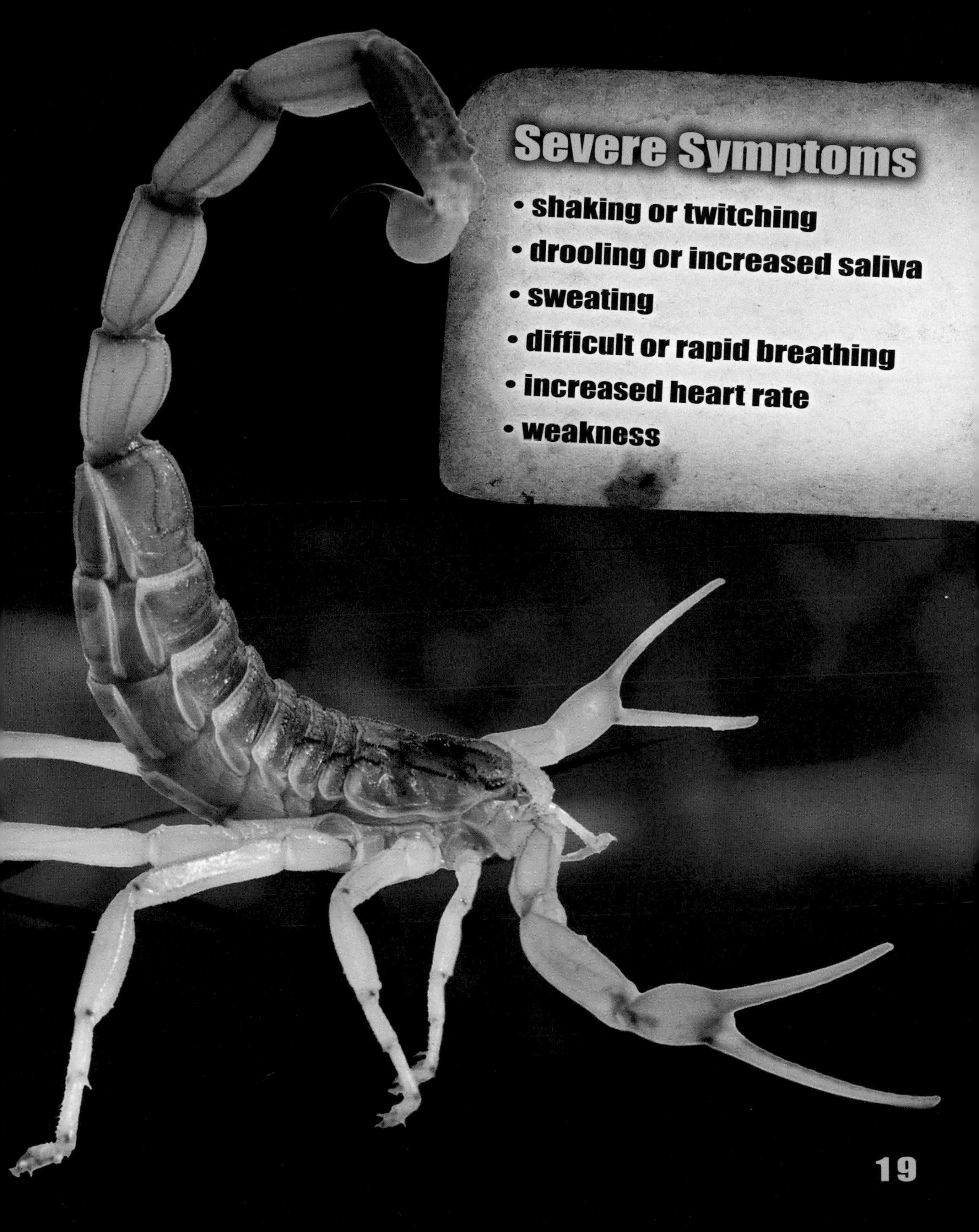

Severe Symptoms

- shaking or twitching
- drooling or increased saliva
- sweating
- difficult or rapid breathing
- increased heart rate
- weakness

Attack Facts

- One sting from a deathstalker scorpion can be enough to kill a human.
- The deathstalker and other scorpions are thought to sting up to 1 million people each year.

Deathstalker venom may be designed to kill. However, it may also have the power to save lives. Chlorotoxin is one of the **toxins** in deathstalker venom. It binds to certain **cancer** cells. It also helps keep them from spreading. Scientists are currently researching ways that deathstalker venom could be used to treat brain cancer.

People all over the world are fascinated by the deathstalker scorpion. Its survival skills are incredible. The strength of its venom is widely feared. If you ever meet a deathstalker in the wild, remember that deadly things can come in small packages.

Glossary

aggressive—violent or threatening

antivenom—a substance that acts against venom and treats the effects of a venomous bite

arachnids—bugs with eight legs and bodies that are divided into two sections; scorpions, spiders, and ticks are arachnids.

burrows—digs a tunnel or hole in the ground

cancer—a disease in which some cells in the body grow faster than normal and destroy healthy tissues; cancer affects different parts of the body and can be deadly.

consciousness—the state of being awake and able to think

inject—to insert fluid into the body through a sharp point

lethal—deadly

nervous system—the body system that is made up of the brain, spinal cord, and nerves

paralyzed—unable to move or feel

pincers—the pinching claws of animals such as scorpions, lobsters, and crabs

toxins—poisonous substances produced by living organisms

ultraviolet—a type of light that humans cannot see; scorpions glow under ultraviolet light.

venom—poison produced by some animals to kill or paralyze prey

venomous—producing a poisonous substance called venom

To Learn More

At the Library

Long, Denise. *Survivor Kid: A Practical Guide to Wilderness Survival*. Chicago, Ill.: Chicago Review Press, 2011.

Markle, Sandra. *Scorpions: Armed Stingers*. Minneapolis, Minn.: Lerner, 2011.

Riehecky, Janet. *Scorpions: On the Hunt*. Mankato, Minn.: Capstone Press, 2010.

On the Web

Learning more about scorpions is as easy as 1, 2, 3.

1. Go to www.factsurfer.com.

2. Enter "scorpions" into the search box.

3. Click the "Surf" button and you will see a list of related Web sites.

With factsurfer.com, finding more information is just a click away.

The images in this book are reproduced through the courtesy of: Stephen Dalton/Photo Researchers, Inc., front cover, p. 17; Imagemore/SuperStock, p. 5; PhotoStock-Israel/Alamy, p. 6; Lance Cpl. Andrew J. Good, p. 8; TSgt Samuel Bendet, p. 9; Daniel Heuclin/naturepl.com, pp. 10, 18-19; Anatolii Kokoza, pp. 12-13; John Bell, pp. 14-15; Matt Reinbold, p. 16; Alessandro Mancini/Alamy, pp. 20-21.